WHO DOESN'T BELIEVE IN MIRACLES IS NOT A REALIST

My Adventuresome Professional Path to Freedom

Author: Laura Milde

Imprint

© Laura Milde 2019

First Edition

Contact: Laura Milde-Borgs

Marienwerderstr. 4a, D-83313 Siegsdorf

wildemilde.com

Mail: info at Laura–Milde.com

Cover art: Laura Milde

Cover photo: Laura Milde

Photographer: Mira Horn

Description

Career success is often longed for, but is granted to very few.

The required large investments put the brakes on many talented people who want to start their own business. Gifts, talents, and abilities are left by the wayside. Laura Milde knows the road from the bottom to the very top. She shares her experiences mercilessly, authentically, warns of pitfalls along the way, and shows possibilities, and how "the little guy" can also fulfill his dream, and how women, even with children, can build interesting, lucrative businesses right at home with minimal expenses. This information can be a blessing for all senior citizens, because many pensioners do not have a sufficient livelihood in their retirement years, actually a very valuable time when one should be able to realize one's wishes and dreams.

The added gift of this exceptional professional career is the personal development and self-unfolding. The result often is that one receives in addition to a lucrative income, a charismatic glow, a self-assured step, and a happy life.

Table of Contents

Preface.. 7

Imprinting and Evil Dogma 9

The Search and the False Answers 11

I Am Successful, therefore I Am 13

Better Questions, New Answers 17

A New Beginning 22

The Impossible Offer 24

The Scent of Freedom....................................... 26

My New Life.. 28

Courage Is Part of It.. 31

My World Becomes Wide 34

Old Dream, Issued Anew................................... 38

An Astonishing Encounter................................. 42

More Villa Mansion than Wooden House 45

My Team Partners Have to Grow Up 48

There Is No Turning Back 50

Christmas Eve Alone in South Tyrol................. 53

Daily Life in South Tyrol.................................. 54

The Flip Side of My Dream............................... 56

An Acquisition in Unknown Territory............... 58

New People, New Places 60

A Little Spoiler 65

What Is Your Profession? 66

The Shock, and Being Done 68

A Recent Descent Before Victory..................................... 85

And Once Again, My New Life... 89

Thank You 94

Extract of "Your Radiant, New I"..................................... 95

Liability Exclusion.. 99

Preface

Like many girls I dreamed of a brilliant future. Only my dream was not to become a princess, a dancer, or an actress like my mother and grandmother. ("Naturally," I studied drama at Mozarteum in Salzburg.) I wanted to become "rich." I wanted to buy the house in Nonn, where I was so happy as a child, (where we were evicted because we couldn't afford it) and gift it to my parents "when I am grown up."

I imagined how my kids would have everything they wished. I would travel and be able to maintain a household at the same time. And I would be able to afford the best piano teacher, not such a "strict, impatient old woman" like I had, (in my child's eyes), but who charged only 5 D-Mark per hour.

I forgot the dream and lived my life. Only after years of existential anxiety, of not knowing how I would pay the next month's rent, and fearing the walk to the mailbox, because (I felt) "nothing but bills" were in it, there awakened in me a spite, a definite will, to change something. No, I wasn't going to become a "tight wad" my whole life and pinch every penny, and still never have enough. I wanted success! I wanted to be "rich!"

I was ready to do all it took. I wanted to work hard and earn "it" for myself. I didn't know at that time, that it also could all go very easily.

Today I don't work hard anymore, rather "for the fun of it," and for this am successful, fulfilled, and have time for the things that are important in my life (like playing piano, mountain climbing, and travel).

If you, like many women, have a project close to your heart, for which you still don't have the necessary capital to invest, then my discovery could also be something for you. Likewise if you simply want more time with your family, you want to see your children and grandchildren grow up, but as a manager you now spend 60 – 70 hours a week at the office and in meetings: A hearty welcome! Or if you just plain have had your fill of thoughts of how to make "precious money," you have no idea how you are going to pay off your apartment or house, and it becomes instantly clear to you: there has got to be another way. Maybe my path will inspire you. You must not make the same mistakes I made.

If you have any questions, find me!

Sometimes it helps to get a recommendation, or networking with interesting people.

Would be nice to meet you.

In Unity,

Laura

Imprinting and Evil Dogma

My little three years old simply did not wake up after an extensive, difficult operation. I cried, I prayed, I cursed, until exhausted, I gave up and said to God, "Please, God in heaven, take my son to you. I cannot take anymore. I give him back to you."

At this moment I heard several nurses call: "Simon has awakened, Simon is conscious again!"

That was my moment of surrender. Still, years of searching would follow, because I didn't really know HIM. I knew nothing of the father-love of God, of HIS love and goodness. And nothing about God's will that life be successful, happy, and healthy – also for me.

Raised Catholic at a boarding school for young English women, with fear of punishment, purgatory, and hell instead of love, I could only imagine God as a threatening power. I happily went to church on Sunday, and came out annoyed and downright disturbed after the priest made it clear to us once again in his thundering sermon, how sinful and bad we all were.

Maybe you remember similar occurrences. In addition, the bigotry struck me, with which the churchgoers piously participated, and after mass ran off at the mouth in front of the church and wholeheartedly devoted themselves to small town gossip.

9

Having grown up, I converted from the Catholic to the Evangelical Church, because I expected more openness and unity with the parishioners. To take the Lord's Supper together in a circle held a certain mystique for me and I took it on myself to become closer to the God of Martin Luther. Yet here also I could not find a spiritual home.

The Search and the False Answers

Like so many in my generation, I embarked on a search into the esoteric scene, relied on the effectiveness of precious stones, and studied the principles of feng shui, spoke daily affirmations like: "I am a money-magnet," to which my subconscious always reacted, "And what do you dream about at night?" And I tried to establish the future by means of horoscopes. I continually attended presentations, practiced mastering life's demands through practicing Silva-Mind-Control. I watered my flowers only after full moons, got my hair cut only on "Leo" days, and tried to influence my daily life through positive thoughts. While I was still up to my ears in problems and didn't know anymore how to help myself, I went to hypnosis, completed three years of psychotherapy, and being a suicide risk, took the drugs that were prescribed to me.

Somehow, the positive affirmations, the self-discipline, the extensive reading of positive self-help literature, the concerning myself with moon cycles, biorhythms, and meditation over a candle all helped me somehow. But it was a struggle, an ongoing battle. True, unbridled joy was an exception in my daily life. Over my life hung a thick fog that obscured everything, Even joyous occasions carried an undertone of anxiety.

Then I flew to America and visited the Mastery-University of Anthony Robbins. He was the Guru in the self-mastery field. I was ready to embark on this journey, to invest a lot of money to overcome my anxieties and to seize on this unfamiliar adventure.

Among ten thousand people spread over two huge halls, strictly guarded by ushers who granted access to the toilets only after permission, because people like to use excuses when it comes to difficult topics.

So, my willingness to bring about a turning point in my life was huge.

I even completed a walk over hot, burning coals, and thought, now I can master anything after conquering my fear of burning myself by emerging at the end of the several meters long burning carpet intact and not burned.

I learned to eat "correctly," drank filtered water by the liter, paid attention to my fitness, and trained to think positively on a daily basis, and I spoke with a fervent positive affirmation. "Now I am the voice! I will lead not follow!" But my voice remained shrill, my daily life heated and driven, if always increasing in success. Yes, I led! Yes, I was heard! But inside me was this anxiety. As soon as I was alone in the house without any connections, I was overwhelmed by the panic feelings and, just exhausted, fell into a fitful sleep.

I Am Successful, therefore I Am

On the outside, I functioned. My cosmetics practice ran like clockwork, I earned good money, a not so simple task for a small cosmetician in this type of business. I simply gave everything I had. I continually attended continuing education courses, improved my products, beautified the space at my practice, bought new and better equipment, and expanded my inventory to include body care products, used exquisite products, and incorporated color and style analysis in my program. For all these additional accomplishments I attended a training institute and earned the requisite certificates.

Through a good customer, I learned of a position for a trainer of young sales people in the area of business practices and self-assured appearance, proper style of clothing and etiquette.

I applied and was awarded the contract. For three and a half years I held monthly courses for the young sales people, earned very good money, and learned a great deal myself. At this time my horizons broadened enormously! I was infected by the great visions among the leaders, with which I led ever more courageous discussions. Yes, it demanded all my courage to keep from making myself small and hiding out as a "little cosmetician." Women in particular tended to talk down their talents and abilities and to fear conversations with "scary monsters." Do you still see this at times today?

I always set higher goals for myself. The tempo of my life was always increasing. I think I did not even notice how I was numbing myself with success, new challenges, all the bling that goes with these, and my own pride. I outdid myself. To feel was painful – and that was easily avoided on my success-trip.

My cosmetic studio continued on well. I made a daring escape from my lower level space into a large, bright space on the first floor of a city villa in the park-like development.

I now had 80 square meters available to me and I fully indulged my passion for unusual interior design. There was a small Solarium, and extra waiting room, and an extensive showroom lined with large windows. I didn't choose ordinary studio facilities, rather colorful showcases, giant pictures, and abundant open space. It was a joy to receive my customers here. I was blessed, and enjoyed this beautiful, colorful ambiance in the middle of a garden. During a transaction I could look out into the tree beyond the window, which gave me a deep inner peace, a sense that carried into my customer in a beneficial way.

In good weather, I took my midday break on the balcony, surrounded by trees, listening to the birds and watching the squirrels. A little idyl in the city. My customers referred people and my client base grew ever larger, to my great enjoyment. Meanwhile well-known names found themselves on my client list and I remember many nice occasions when I encountered "Mrs Normaluser," a famous actress, in my studio.

And still, the work didn't satisfy me as it had in the first years. And for this reason I devoted myself to the books again, and "built" my great Naturopathic Practice at the Center for Natural Healing in Munich. In the subject of homeopathy, I found myself quite at home and studied Hahnemann backwards and forwards, studied repertorisation at the Kent Repertorium, and also drove weekly to the Homeopathy School at Gauting, near Munich. I was quite proud that I passed my Naturopath Exam on the first try, a significant accomplishment, given the 80% failure rate.

I studied voraciously and put into practice everything I learned, because my cosmetics clients gladly and openly accepted my new expertise. For my patients who received a homeopathic consultation, there was a separate room available, which I neatly appointed with a corner desk and a writing table as well as bookcases along an entire wall for all my textbooks. During the consultation my coaching talent crystalized over time, and what had begun as a homeopathic consult often became a coaching conversation. I always had an open ear for my cosmetics clients, and now I would, with an open heart and open spirit, lead people to their very own wisdom living inside them. Through recommendations I was invited to presentations and my working circle became ever larger, to my great joy. In addition, I was captivated by the study of constitutionals and typology in homeopathy, because I found in the books my own peculiarities described, and so felt less like an outsider. I sometimes wondered, "How does the author of this book know me so well?" I could pretty much relate myself to a certain remedy, something for which I held great fascination.

Indeed, I was caught on a rat race, even if it was golden on the surface. The rent has to be figured in, operating costs reined in, and the inventory expanded. Every day I packed the laundry basket with dirty laundry into the car, because I didn't want a washing machine in the bath at the practice. It would have spoiled my sensitivity to the chic ambience of the place. Having arrived at home after an hour drive, depending where I lived at the time, the work continued. Do the wash, dry it and store it, put the laundry basket back in the car, update the cash book, prepare bookkeeping, order products, book continuing education, arrange terms with representatives, and wrap up conversations with patients. Thank God I only offered my practice to private patients; otherwise I would have sat for many more hours billing insurance companies. This recommendation by the school was worth its weight in gold, because I often hear complaints about this from colleagues.

Better Questions, New Answers

One day I stood in front of my practice with a full laundry basket and asked myself, "How much longer are you willing to put up with all this stress?" This question opened a new realm for me, which will receive greater emphasis later.

To develop myself further was my hobby horse, and so I completed many seminars by noteworthy trainers, invested in myself and my expertise, and read all possible texts that held promise for my personal growth. My father, from whom I have inherited my fervor for books, believed I should read biographies and good novels, something I didn't allow myself at that time. I was too busy trying to improve my life, develop my personality, and promote my education. In any case, I read biographies of rich, successful people in order to profit from their wisdom. I also thank my father for this striving for self-development, because he was the one who brought me to my first seminar. He had heard of a course which included teachings on thought control, and this fascinated him. So he invited me to attend this three day seminar, Silva Mind Control, along with him. We attended three sequential Trainings, which were very meaningful for me, as I had a very intense exchange with him, and also learned to apply this material to my life.

At Pallas Seminar I learned an enormous amount about life. Very actionable methods that helped me through the years to master my life. With humor and catchy cartoons the Pallas Seminar Leader conveyed conducive knowledge, a greater understanding, and a deep sense of gratitude. Here I came in contact with the "discipline of gratitude." I recognized that the greater gratitude I perceived for all the good in my life, the more blessings were drawn into my life. For me, Alfred Stielau-Pallas was a very enriching and compelling encounter. Further, he was a link to my mother, who had committed suicide, taking me down to untold emotional depths as a result. Alfred Stielau-Pallas was a client of my mother, who initially narrated for him his seminars on cassettes, on account of her professional qualifications as an actress. Still today, I have one of these cassettes, a priceless memento of the wonderful, richly accented voice of my mother.

In one of his seminars I learned the unbelievably helpful exercise of imagining that my mother's suicide was a true gift for my life, something that was once impossible for me to think. Over the years I have come to understand that this imaginary bypass has made possible a new perspective on this tragic event, as well as a focus away from poor victim to an open spirit who always seeks the good, the beautiful, and the beneficial.

Here I also learned to have a greater understanding for people and their weaknesses, including my own. The most helpful imagery here is of a skyscraper, in which I imagine climbing from the basement to the tenth floor. From the basement floor, I see only the feet of passersby, who toddle their way down the sidewalk. From the ground floor I see people, cars, and bicycles rushing by. From the window of the second floor I see the trees beside the road, the sun splashed colorfully on the balconies of the houses across the street. From the fifth floor I can overlook the entire park, see the garden from above, and the children playing in the sandboxes on the playground across the way. And finally, arriving at the tenth floor, I can enjoy the wide view, the mountains and maybe a lake in the distance.

Thus also grows the understanding of one's own life and personal development, a spiritual ascent, so to speak. I could also make the observation that the wiser and more successful a person is, the higher in the skyscraper they have climbed, the friendlier and more understanding these encounters were for me.

One seminar I must definitely mention, because it fascinated, excited, and lifted me up so much, that I attended it eight times. Yes, eight times. It is the Forum of Landmark Education. It was always notorious for being "mega-American," and was supposedly a cult. One seminar leader introduced himself with the words, "Excuse me for being an American and for being too American." That hit me deeply and I grasped which prejudices had almost held me back from using this wonderful win-producing seminar for myself. It could not be a cult, because the signs of a cult are that you pray to a "guru," you give yourself up, you spend a lot of money, and you contribute your work skills for free. In the forum, the people were enabled to think independently, to be conscious of their whole power, and encouraged and guided to live in peace with all people. And it was cheaper by far than many other similar seminars that I attended, especially since the repetitions were possible for a small fee. So, for me, what really hit home and what I still use today and remember in difficult situations are the "Distinctions," (Exercises) that enable me to master challenges with gallant charm. I am happy and grateful that this forum was still available in Munich at that time. I don't know if it is even still available to book in Germany, and far be it from me to provide advertisements for any of my completed education. I have been very pleased by the ideas of "self mastering" and discipline. I always have a choice of how circumstances affect me. I always have a choice how I react to situations. And it became clear to me, that the meanings of certain experiences were added by myself, and I cannot blame anyone. The end of the victim-existence, then! You can't taste this just one time. Just the responsibility for taking everything on feels stressful for the first time. It is an absolute requirement, just to have power over one's life, to master challenges without hanging onto complaints, and to courageously change the things that no longer fit in one's life concept. Only I myself can master or change my life circumstances. When I assign blame, I give up equally my power and my autonomy. Freedom is born of the acceptance of self- responsibility. Freedom is the gift of not taking oneself too seriously, yet at the same time recognizing one's true greatness within, and the greatness in others. I took the assignment "to climb down" literally, placed myself on a chair, and consciously climbed down, which, in a translated sense, is a relinquishing of one's rights. So my cells and I became conscious, in that I (often at first!) climbed down from a chair, a wall, sometime a table if necessary, in especially stubborn cases; that freedom lies in giving up your need to be right. As we say in Bavaria, "You're right. I have my peace." Or the idea: "You're either right or successful!"

A New Beginning

I often told myself "my story" from poor victim until I realized that it is exactly that: a story! And stories can be invented, rearranged, and rewritten. When I then learned that our brains play tricks on us, and that our memories often have nothing to do with the original event, I had to laugh, and began to rewrite my childhood with the motto, "It is never too late for a happy childhood."

Looking back, I can say that, all in all, it has paid off to invest in myself and my growth. All the books read and pored over often with a pen light, all the scripts brought home after seminars, conscientiously reviewed, all the cassettes, CDs, and presentations, have had a deep effect on me. I felt better, mastered my challenges elegantly, and related to myself as I am today and not who I had to be, according to my past. My car became a rolling university – an image I retained from Nikolaus Enkelmann, whom I remember as a great person and a wise trainer. Just recently I remembered, it was Enkelmann who asked the question, "Are you courageous enough to ask yourself the question: God, what do you have planned for me?" At that time I didn't understand the wisdom in this question. But it shows that the cells remember everything; that in due time, a sentence, a picture, an idea crops up when we come to a fork in life's road for example, or when we must make a big decision, or when we inwardly are asking for help.

I remained a searcher. I felt I had not yet arrived. There must be something else there. This can't be all there is. You are also familiar with this – the thoughts, the unrest, the striving, right? Yes, I was by all appearances further along on my success trip. And I was supposed to scale new heights of professional success. Through my inner unrest, my perception remained awake.

The Impossible Offer

And so, one day I recognized THE opportunity that I saw on a business form, something I had never heard of before. I learned from a VHS, a video cassette – yes, it was that long ago – an exciting system in which money was not earned as a result of individual effort, but rather together with people, in a team! For me as a sole proprietor, this was electrifyingly new. I studied every word and took apart the whole offer and set aside the cassettes. Too new, too rare, too exciting, this description of the business model.

But it rumbled inside me. This idea would not let go of me. I took hold of my heart and picked up the phone, and dialed the number provided in the literature. They weren't ready to explain anything over the phone, and now that I was at the peak of curiosity, they invited me to an event in a nearby hotel.

What awaited me there blew away my readiness to take in what I'd read as the truth. Too garish, too loud, too aggressive, all of it inundated me. I was supposed to meet some "crazy, successful people" and decide immediately on a new, great business and ideally, sign somewhere. I fled!

But the seed was sown. When one day a good customer of my cosmetic institute told me all excitedly of a new business idea, I was open. If anything, she must assure me that it was not the "loud, garish company" from which I had recoiled in horror. I wanted to know more. Again I was invited to an event, a business presentation as I had been told. I was pleasantly surprised by the business like appearance of the people, the quiet, and the clearly structured message on the overhead. This time I understood much better how a compensation plan can function. And above all, no one pressured me at all, they gave me the time I needed to think about this innovative system as a business opportunity.

The Scent of Freedom

As it concerned a 5,000 D-Mark investment for the initial product package, that I could test and use and learn to present, I saved up a quick shot. The business was in magnetic products, like sleep systems, sports bandages, and shoe inserts, water filters and air filters. I got involved in the material through books about magnetic field therapy, went to presentations on it, and read everything I could get my hands on about this network marketing idea. What a fascinating idea, to make money collectively, with a team, for the benefit of each. Everyone brings her own performance to the team, recommends and sells the product further, and can even recommend the business model to a person seeking a second income. I could not stop thinking, "What if this were really possible?" It would fulfill my dream of being able to work anywhere, not just in one place like at my practice, tied to one place. I could not take my clients and patients with me to another city. Though I have moved many times in my life, but for 20 years had my practice in East Munich, I had to take into account the drive time from my house at that time. At that time I lived in Avenhausen, not far from Marquartstein, then moved near Augsburg, to the hinterland of Aichach, then back to Aschau in the Chiemgau. Every morning I needed over an hour in the car on a good day, unless a traffic jam would slow me down at the Irschenberg nerve center or, coming from the opposite direction, the Eschenrieder bottleneck. And after close of business, the same thing on the way back. Even if I used the time well by listening to interesting audio books, it was a challenge that became heavier and harder to master over the years. And in the end it cost me not only my nerves, but also the incumbent high car expenses. Then there was not only my need to move where I liked, but also my longstanding wish to emigrate to Italy, and my always still listening to company presentations and the chance for financial freedom. They even spoke of passive, or residual income, enticing for me as a sole proprietor, but unimaginable.

What I understood was, that how much money I earned, depended on my own commitment. And yes, I could work! I had done so for years. And likewise, I was used to getting involved in new areas of interest. I could come up with several professional titles. But each of my independent initiatives demanded my full commitment: personal and ongoing. And with network marketing it was supposed to be possible to build a team over the years and to thereby generate residual income. What a grandiose idea. Too good to pass up. I jumped, and invested what was for me a large sum, because in addition the inventory, there were several other costs for a license, catalogs, seminars, and entry fees to business presentations that I attended several times a week with other interested people.

My New Life

"A magic lives inside every new beginning, one that protects us and helps us to live," as Hermann Hesse has written.

An exciting time followed. Exciting, work intensive, hectic, and very, very successful. I began to tell everyone that I had started a new business and invited those who were interested to attend information sessions, because I was not yet able to explain the business model myself. After seeing a hundreds of presentations at nearby hotels, I was in a position to give the business presentation myself. And that is, what I enthusiastically did at my beautiful business space. Thank God I learned fast and trusted myself to speak in front of people. I also invited clients and patients because they remarked about a positive change they noticed in me and wondered what the reason for it was. I was positively charged, full of confidence to do the right thing, to make a difference in people's lives and to gain financial independence for myself. I also made a few faux pas, as I exuberantly told of my own financial goals that I had set. I can remember well a banker who thought I was crazy when I told him about the income possibilities in this branch. With time and all my continuing education and training, I have learned not to spook people in my exuberance, and to not "feed them with a firehose." I learned to listen more, and find out what the needs of potential candidates were, and learned that many people likewise long for freedom and independence.

I worked hard. Practically every free moment between two businesses, I phoned people to invite them to info sessions. After closing, I kept the doors open to those interested in my new business. I showed the products, showed how they worked; I drew circles to explain the compensation plan. On the way home I listened to cassettes in order to improve my know-how and to raise my mindset to a higher level.

My former husband regarded me with skepticism. He could not ignore my increased energy, my elan, my joy at continually climbing in our compensation plan. And money was coming in, increasingly. It was the proof that my plan had worked. That's why he was ready to "let me run."

And all at once I was "on top." I was a Diamond, a leadership level in this company. I earned many times as much as I did at my cosmetic and naturopathic practice, and shrewdly decided to sell it. I advertised in *der Beauty*, informed business colleagues, and finally found a young woman who was brave enough to open her own studio right after completing her cosmetology training. Since she could take on the client list, and the space was big enough for her to live in as well, we agreed on the sale. She got the whole works for an economy-price, like we say "an apple and an egg," and because I was longing for my freedom to work from anywhere, I wanted to be done with the deal. I was determined to completely close this chapter of my life, and I left it with just my handbag in hand.

My clients could not believe it. It stroked my ego considerably, when so many of my clients asked whether I could handle them privately, and for many women there were tears at our parting. But my plan could not be implemented if I had one foot in the past. I wanted to get up and out and was ready to do everything necessary for this. Friends recommended that I set up a little studio in my home, just in case my new project didn't go as well as planned. Yes, the idea was tempting, and I also loved this work. There was enough space in the house, even with a guest bath in the addition. But I let go of the idea, because I had committed all resources to my new career, and wanted to put all my eggs in one basket. My decision stood firm: I would achieve "it" and not waste any thoughts on any possible setbacks.

Courage Is Part of It

I look back today and recognize that I had such great success, because I so clearly set my goals, was ready to do all it took, and to "burn all ships behind me." That included the readiness to flush out and let go of old, outdated dogmas and to replace them with new, beneficial thoughts. My mindset required a remolding! My boarding school education by the nuns inoculated my every cell with limiting patterns. I internalized, that humility was for show, that all worldly things were reprehensible, and that it was easier for a camel to pass through the eye of a needle, than it was for a rich man to enter heaven. Such a misinterpretation of this well-known bible verse! So, it was no wonder that my striving for success was always associated with a bad conscience, and that I always would place obstacles in my way. I managed a pretty well functioning sabotage-program! Because success at least had to be gained through hard work and was not in any case to be reached easily. And then there was the experience of my childhood, when money was hard to earn and huge sums of money were only available to the rich – "the bigshots." We lived in a little house on a sunny slope in Nonn, outside of Bad Reichenhall. I loved to play at the edge of the woods, romp around the expansive garden with my dog, Kito, pick wildflowers, or in winter, to be able to skate from right outside the front door. My father had built me a treehouse in which I slept in the summer, my own room. A fairytale dream comes true for me, for which I am forever grateful to my father. As the house was going to be sold, and my

31

parents didn't have the means, we had to leave our "little house." Out of the dream! For 30,000 D-Mark! This "eviction" from our home, paradise for me, stuck deeply in my tender girl's soul. I grasped it: We were those in hand me down clothes, who just didn't have "it" in them. We would surely get into heaven! Only until that happened, I would work hard, so that my children and I would be spared such a fate. My stubborn Capricorn-pighead would help me to reach the unreachable.

My team grew, as did my capabilities. I liked the people and invested myself in them. I was on task; whenever they needed me I called, offered to meet in my space, and drove at least weekly to hotel events.

A very grand reward was my Diamond celebration in London, at the Tower Bridge. I was supposed to give a small speech in English, as there were attendees from around the world. I was already used to speaking in public, but my English was still not good enough to give a speech, especially one, that is spontaneous and off the cuff.

I took the challenge and said, "Dare to make mistakes!" That was my message. I was astounded by the applause, but I had been told that it's exactly this message networkers must take to heart. Oh yes, I had made big mistakes. I have demanded too much from my team members, many had "put up" with me for too long, and for others I had not recognized their potential. I learned that everyone has their own approach, that I should not impose all my "wild art," and that you can't teach a cat to bark! The only important thing was to learn from mistakes and, if possible, not to repeat them.

My World Becomes Wide

My first big incentive was a trip to Hawaii. Oh, how big and wide my world had become iridescent, bling-bling. A first stop was in Australia. Sidney impressed me, in part because I could hardly get lost in this city, so square to the ruler were the streets, at least in the area of our hotel. I discovered a store, "The Cashmere House," where there were extensive rooms with hundreds of cashmere shawls in every color. For me, an El Dorado. I bought! Oh, I enjoyed the feeling of having enough money. I still remember big shawls, fluffy scarves, and a stole from this shopping trip. It was a very special experience for me to simply indulge in the desire to buy things because of their beauty, not because I needed them.

Hawaii was so special and exciting, as I always had imagined it. We were picked up at the airport in a large bus. When boarding, we were each presented with necklaces of fresh flowers, and welcomed with "Aloha," and a small bow. This charming ritual put me at ease in this new and strange world. I was excited! Exuberant, we stormed the beach and attacked the waves on our first evening. But I regretted this carelessness, because the sea was wilder than I had imagined, and I swallowed a lot of water and even sand, and came back to the beach scared, snorting, and beating wildly about myself. In the future I would be more careful in unfamiliar terrain.

But the next day the ordeal was quickly forgotten, because we were spoiled all around with delicious food, magical music, and generous gifts. And as is typical for many women to get a new hair style for a big event, I went to the nearest hairdresser, recommended by the receptionist, and had my hair trimmed short.

The time in Hawaii gave wings to my business. Back home again, I could tell such wonderful stories from my trip, that my team partners set their sights higher and also wanted to go on these adventures. And so, I had a full calendar, I supported my team partners where I could, and enjoyed the successes of the top people on my team.

Just reaching Diamond status in my company was a great feeling. But even more exciting and exhilarating was to congratulate my first diamond couple. I always liked to be on stage. I enjoyed the attention, the applause, the goodwill of the people, and the recognition of my success. But leaving the stage to my leader was just magical. I was so happy that I could not stop cheering, clapping, and expressing my congratulations. Because with the great success of the Diamond pair, many ranks have been achieved by partners from their team. That is the beauty and magic in network marketing: Your own success is only possible through the success of "your people" on the team. Win-win in its purest form. And that everyone has the opportunity to achieve a leadership position is a real gift. Of course, it requires commitment, the will to succeed, diligence, the willingness to follow and learn, and not everyone is ready for it. But it is possible! In a large enterprise, however, working up from "assembly line worker" to CEO is not possible, or like the American Dream, a rare exception.

But there are also dangers that come with great success. I earned so much money that I treated myself every time I went on a business trip. At the airport the exclusive shops lured with Aigner, Gucci, Hermes, etc., and for the first time in my life I had no worries about money. Quite the opposite: I lived in excess! I could get an Aigner bag for 800 D-Mark or a Hermes towel for 500 D-Mark or more. Since I worked quite a bit and hardly ever came to the city, the airport was a shopping paradise for me.

Since I also donated from my abundance to less privileged people, I had no guilty conscience for finally treating myself so well.

That was not really the problem. When I became arrogant, I found myself abominable. I saw an Aigner bag in a shop window and I wanted it, so I went into the shop and asked the saleswoman to give me the bag out of the window. She handed me the bag and gave me the price, to which I replied, "I wanted to buy the bag and not know the price!" Peeved, the saleswoman packed up the bag and as soon as I stepped out of the store, I felt sorry. No, I didn't want to be like this! Thankfully, I noticed in time that I was about to become a disgusting bitch, and changed my posture immediately after this incident. Deep gratitude was actually more natural for me, for I had never forgotten where I had come from. Although there was always enough food in my parents' house, I can not quite understand how my father did it. It was always a struggle to pay bills and due to this, the house blessing hung a little crooked. To really afford something that was not necessarily vital was at times out of the question as were "little pleasures" like a visit to the cinema or coffee and cake at the *Café Spieldiener*.

Old Dream, Issued Anew

Not only the abundance of money was new to me. The independence was particularly attractive. At last I could imagine following my dream to move to Italy. I paged through bright brochures, read travel logs, and collected all sorts of information on my favorite country: Italy. I also improved my Italian skills through courses, and I dreamed of sandy beaches and winding streets, wide promenades, spaghetti and the best vino rosso. Bella Italia!

As I talked about it more and more with my father and with my girlfriends, it became apparent that I was too cowardly for Bella Italia. The culture shock would be too big, and there would be too many cuts from the familiar and hard won life that I would have to make. So I came to South Tyrol. That would be a few hours from Munich, so that my friends would be able to come visit, and I could drive off to Munich more often still. Here I would also indulge my passion for hiking, and my dogs would be happy as long as the summers wouldn't be too crazy hot. Besides, I loved the hearty food, and I could also get red wine and spaghetti here. One spoke German here, and that gave me an element of added security, and I could still "execute" my Italian.

On a beautiful day in October, I drove to Bressanone with my father to look at apartments and houses for rent there.

We went outside of Bressanone to eat at Nats in a tavern and asked the owner whether he knew anything about where to rent a house or apartment. We thought it would be easiest to ask the locals first. We found them very helpful. We were to wait a bit, then someone would call someone about a place to rent. After a snack and a tasty beer, we were fortified by what was to come. Into the dining room came a man who probably had just come from the stable, for the smell of the stable was clearly perceptible from our table. After a wordy welcome in South Tyrolese, of which we understood hardly anything, the farmer came directly to us, sat down next to me, and told us enthusiastically about his wood house, which stood empty now, and he would be happy to show it to us. To my ears, that sounded absolutely wonderful. Because that's exactly what I had in mind: to live in perfect peace out in the country in the most beautiful, natural surroundings with my dogs and cats, to drive to nearby Bressanone now and then, and to build a new life here for myself. For this I gladly accepted the intense "fragrance" of animals and nature in the bargain.

We could go with him right away and he would show us everything. We were only too happy to go with him. But it was a surprise to us that we should ride with him on his tractor. We offered to drive our van and bring him back to the tavern. So, we got in the van and drove about 15 minutes after which we were standing in front of a hut in not so good condition. THAT was supposed to be the wood house for rent? This was exactly the idea of our charming, fragrant companion. You could do a lot of fixing up, which was not a problem. The basic substance of the place was good, there were electric lights and running water and a functioning wood burning stove would heat the whole house. Puh! I had other ideas. The location was magical! A wide view over the country, meadows all around, fruit trees and a somewhat overgrown garden enchanted me. Just the idea of setting up this hovel with my antique furniture was grotesque.

We explained that it was probably out of the question, something Seppi, whose name we learned, could not understand. We drove back to the restaurant, thanked Seppi and the host for a free beer, and headed for Bressanone. We would have the smell of the stalls in the car for a bit longer, which made us laugh spontaneously when we were out of sight. We followed one more tip and drove to another mountain village where an apartment in a farmhouse was for rent. An open minded and sympathetic woman showed us the apartment, which was in a "Zuhausel," a small house near the main building. The tranquility, the broad, surrounding fields and the breathtaking mountain views inspired me. But then the problem was that I would bring two dogs with me, which that landlord, the farmer, didn't want, as he feared that his sheep, cows, chickens and ducks would be hunted by the dogs.

I knew, of course, that my dogs would never do that, since I had Shapendoes, Dutch sheep dogs, who would herd the sheep but never hunt them. The farmer said that dog owners would always say two sentences: "The dog does nothing," and "Oh, he has never done that." I had to laugh and we said goodbye with a laugh and also a crying eye of the sympathetic farm folk.

In Bressanone we strolled across the Adler Bridge to the Cathedral Square and suddenly found ourselves in front of a large sign of a real estate agent, who had his domicile right next to the Cathedral of Bressanone. Now, maybe that was a sign, but it was normal to go through a broker to find a house or apartment in the Bressanone area.

An Astonishing Encounter

We found the name tag on the heavy old wooden door of the lordly looking house with turrets and pinnacles. We decided to just give it a try, though we had no proper idea of what we were looking for, exactly.

After we had rung, the buzzer sounded and like Open Sesame, the large wooden door swung open, and then we stood in a stately entrance with a wide wooden staircase that led to the real estate office. The soft creaking of the oiled, wooden steps suggested the long history of this castle-like building. When we arrived upstairs, the surprise was perfect: an artist type awaited us in a perfectly styled outfit, a stylish designer suit, long, well-groomed hair, mirror-polished, pointed shoes, and a broad smile that revealed a row of bright, white teeth. I stared in confusion at this extraordinary materializing of a picture of a man and it was only his amused question if he could somehow help us that brought me to my senses. I think that I stammered when I introduced us and put forward our request. I am usually eloquent and never at a loss for words, but the encounter with this particular gentleman took my breath away. I realized that it was similar for my father. He calculated in his mind how expensive the services of such an office would be. Anyway, I paid.

But now we had landed here and now I would fully enjoy to the fullest this peculiar moment. Afterall, I was trained in acting, and was able to get involved in this game. Of all things, the space into which we were led was phenomenal in its size as well as its furnishings. The opportunity to enter such an extraordinary space did not come by every day. Charmingly and used to admiration, he invited us to just look around, in order to properly arrive. How thoughtful! I accepted the offer and asked if I might look around the room, which was generously allowed with the words, "You may not, only. You must!" This was followed by a narrative of the history of this house, which I have forgotten again. What I will never forget is the impression that this very special facility made on me. I was enchanted by this successful mixture of antique, modern, and downright unusual ideas which were indeed striking, but harmoniously arranged in this spacious room. As a particularly fascinating and funny example, I remember the cupboard whose doors served as the entrance to the toilet. "Our" broker probably had not only a knack for real estate, because the whole placed breathed success, but also a special passion for interior design as well as great creativity. I had to compose myself in the face of these antique and in some cases precious rarities, as well as this extraordinary man who had the courage to implement his ideas, whether in his choice of furnishings or his clothes.

When we sat down and made our request, Mr. F. explained that it was quite abnormal to rent a house in South Tyrol. Normally all the houses were owner occupied and passed down from generation to generation. And so it could not have been just by chance that he could offer us just such a wood house, albeit at 1,000 meters in St. Andrae, above Bressanone, at the foot of the Plose, a mountain well-known for winter sports and hiking. In addition there was the famous Plose water just across the border.

I was excited! From the beginning I found our house hunting excursion to South Tyrol to be blessed and guided. To live at 1,000 meters in a small village had been my dream from the beginning. Also, the story behind this wood house for rent was very special.

He would set up a viewing for us at once and arrange it for the coming day.

We spent that night in Nats, in a pension with a lovely lady who spoiled us with bacon and red wine and entertained us with little stories from the area. Despite all the excitement I slept deeply and soundly, dreaming of expensive mansions, venerable castles and stately men. The next morning, after a sumptuous breakfast and a little walk in the orchards of Nats, it was time. We met at the Cathedral Square with the real estate agent, who could get the owner of the house in St. Andrae to go with us, since we would not be staying very long here in Bressanone.

The trip to St. Andrae was relatively short, just long enough for the landlady to get a picture of me and to ask what moved me to "Emigrate" to South Tyrol. I told her about my long-standing passion for Italy, nature, and my yearning for peace. I would learn soon enough that South Tyrol did not want to be compared with Italy.

More Villa Mansion than Wooden House

My imagination was exceeded by far! I had imagined a wooden cottage, a tiny house with a little garden in front. Little windows with checkered red and white curtains. A bench in front of the house where I would sit with my cat in my lap. But we drove into a wide driveway with a double garage, beside which appeared a large house with large windows on the first floor, a sweeping balcony that led on one side into a garden that nestled around the house. A curved stone staircase led from the door down to the garden. It was so inviting, the garden laid out so charmingly. And yes, there was a bench. It stood under a huge, beautifully grown fir tree. I was delighted! The view swept over the Brixen Valley and across the rugged mountain peaks. How I loved these mountains already! Yes, I would want to live here.

Since the house was built on a hill, there were different levels, which lent the house a special character. Through the double garage, whose door was opened at the push of a button, you came into the sprawling basement rooms of the house. There were shelves attached to the walls everywhere, and a ski boot heater too. Through a door there was a sauna and sunbed. And in a back room there was enough space for a complete workout studio. Up one set of stairs we met the upper floor. Also here, everything inviting and charmingly laid out. A tiled stove, a wooden table with a corner seat gave a rustic touch to the room. In a word: a feel-good house! My excitement pleased the owner and we were agreed that I would get the lease. She trusted the realtor, who assured her that I was the right tenant. He had a good impression of me after we had talked of my career path, and I was also again happy to be financially free and mobile, thanks to my network marketing business.

My father was also thrilled with the location over Bressanone with a view far into the country and the mountains. He just said that the house was too big for me, because I would live in it alone. Well, yes, with my two dogs and two kitties. But since I also lived large in Chiemgau, I had no doubt that I could fill this spacious house with life.

On the way home we discussed all the coincidences that befell us on this crazy act of finding a home on a weekend trip to South Tyrol. We got involved in a set of strange encounters, and we were rewarded. I had somewhat mixed feelings, since my plan had now turned into a fact, but I didn't want to make myself crazy. Everything would continue as well as it had begun. After arriving back home in Chiemgau, I was a little heartsick. I had lived quite magically there in my "Tuscan Villa" with a huge garden and the Schafelbach flowing through it. I had really specially decorated this place, with the open modular kitchen, spacious living room with tall, ceiling height pictures, a white fireplace and my antique piano. Would I put it all in "my wood house?"

But I definitely wanted to do it. For years, I had dreamed of Emigrating to Italy. If I could not at least make it to South Tyrol now at age 50, I would get angry later and "bite a monogram on my behind," I knew. I thought about the sentence that Elizabeth Kubler-Ross said about dying people, "They do not regret what mistakes they made, but what they did NOT implement." Elizabeth Kubler-Ross dealt intensively with dying and what makes it easy or difficult for people when it's time to let go. And I learned from one of my great coaches the idea of judging from the end what is happening in the present. What will I someday wish to say on my deathbed about this situation here today? "I did it!" Not that I was cowardly and tight! But that I would pull it off, no matter the cost!

Afterall, I've always been on the go, doing something completely or not at all. I have often had to show courage in my life and have never regretted my bets. And in order to experience something new in my life, I needed to let go of something old. This was tied to the pain of saying goodbye. I was ready.

My Team Partners Have to Grow Up

There were a few unexpected discussions with partners on my team who did not like the fact that I would not be holding the weekly business presentations anymore. Also there, farewell pain was felt. Abandoning comfort and stepping up into the limelight was unimaginable for many of my team members. But I knew that it was a chance or them to grow and take responsibility. They had heard the presentations and training so often, they could recite them themselves as long as they trusted in themselves. Of course, I would practice with them until they felt safe. Besides, I did not emigrate to Australia. South Tyrol could be reached in about three hours by car, and I would often come to Munich, which also calmed me.

Exactly that was just one of the wonderful benefits of network marketing, to be able to work from anywhere and not be tied down, and for me it was a chance to get involved in the Italian market, something that would place my success on a wider base.

And today we have the advantage of modern technology that can connect us over long distances via Skype, Google-zoom or telephone conferences, and usually it's free! In a Zoom call people meet from kilometers apart, like in a shared living room. This opens up a huge market for us in network marketing, with unimagined possibilities. And people are more and more accustomed to show up on Facebook, Instagram, or other social media and to exchange information there. It is a part of growing to leave behind old, well-trodden paths and to travel new more modern roads. The adage is true: Who does not change with the times, passes, with time. I was not at first so excited about the possibilities of expanding my business via the internet. I had learned that networking is a people business and you can only imagine the business from person to person. Today I am happy about all the young colleagues who grew up with the internet and who inaugurate us "old hands" in the secrets of the technologies and their blessings for our companies. Today, the dream of international business is easier than ever to realize. But getting to know each other personally, building real, loving relationships, and experiencing shared highlights are, of course, the icing on the cake today. The cuddle factor is not to be underestimated. Building strong teams that pull together and work towards a common goal requires true cohesion and a joy in working together. Driving together to a company event is, for example, a great way to get to know each other.

There Is No Turning Back

Now it was time. The truck was at the door and I was more than grateful for the many helpers who helped me pack. My friends were always there when I moved, which I did quite often.

I packed a bunch of odds and ends into the trunk of my big van. I would pick up the dogs and cats later, since they could still stay with a friend in Aschau.

It was snowing heavily when the convoy of trucks, my van, and my ex-husband, who insisted on coming with us in order to help unload, set off in the direction of Bella Italia. Despite snowstorms, we arrived whole in St. Andrae in the evening. The roads were cleared and salted, so the truck safely mastered the serpentine road up to 1,000 meters. I was very happy to finally arrive. We would unload the next day, so we all went down to Milland for a Chinese dinner. There was no shortage of comedy about our having Chinese food in Italy, but it was the first place that caught our eye.

The next morning, after a cold night on makeshift beds in the house, we unloaded the truck and the men distributed the furniture to the rooms where I had designated it.

I drove back down the winding road to Milland, where I went to the grocery store for a fortifying snack. The difference in the range of goods was clear: There were many different types of bacon, sweet breads, pasta of all kinds, and a selection of wines, grappa, liqueurs that was impossible to fully survey. And with Christmas just around the corner, towers of Panettone, a special cake eaten at Christmas time. Here is where I would shop in the future. A strange feeling came over me. On the one hand I felt great anticipation and on the other I felt jittery about all the new and unknown things. Would I be able to settle here? Would I find friends here? Would I be successful here? Many questions whirled in my head and I was happy, once back up in St. Andrae, to be taken in by the activity of moving in and to have no time for indulging in any brooding.

"My men" were properly engaged in their work, making sure I was not left with any temporary, makeshift arrangements. They hung the lamps, put together cabinets, the bed and the bookshelf, and in front of the tiled stove they piled wood that they had found in the adjoining shed. But then, after a lengthy farewell, good wishes and some good advice, I stood alone in the huge house. I had already lived alone in Aschau in Chiemgau for three years, so I was used to it. But I still felt so strange, lonely, and lost here. After all the hustle and bustle of the move, an eerie silence had returned. And soon it would be Christmas. How would I experience spending Christmas Eve alone? But it was my express wish to spend my first Christmas here alone. Somehow I wanted to prove to myself that I could master this.

I rolled up my sleeves and started working through the moving boxes, and began moving everything in. I was glad to be distracted by this work, besides, I had an absolute will to have everything finished, furnished and in a liveable state by Christmas Eve. And I had four full days to do this.

On the day before Christmas Eve, pretty much exhausted from my moving in and cleaning action, I met a neighbor at the fence and introduced myself as the new tenant, and asked her when masses were held the next day. She looked at me uncomprehendingly and said that the Christmas mass was in two days, on the 24th of December. Then I hugged her and thanked her for the greatest gift you can give someone: She had given me a whole day. I had confused the days in the rush and now was nearly done with the unpacking and moving in. Now I could enjoy the preparations in peace. The neighbor responded somewhat disturbed by my emotional outburst, so I learned my first lesson, that South Tyrolers need some time before they warm up to strangers.

Christmas Eve Alone in South Tyrol

My focus is on the message of Christmas. Nothing distracts me. Pure Christmas! "A child is born. A son is given to us." Jesus Christ came into the world to bring us the message of peace. At Christmas is a truce, even in the theaters of war in the world. I feel true Christmas joy and can enjoy being alone. I had never experienced a Christmas Eve alone before and always had had respect for this, because I had always heard of lonely people who felt so lost at Christmas. Now I realize that I myself am "full," full of trust, full of love, full of confidence, and therefore in need of nothing from outside to make me feel whole. And yes, I am happy about my new home that is just newly made ready, decorated nicely for me alone. But then I was not lonely: "Trixi," my tigress, purred in my lap, Sumi, the cat who would have won every beauty contest and knows it, made herself comfortable on the stove bench, and my two dogs, Roxy and her daughter Allyssa, lay at my feet on their sheepskin. Now I was really happy that I had brought my housemates to me before Christmas.

Daily Life in South Tyrol

Also here, daily life returned and with it, new challenges. The registration of my network marketing business was not so simple as in Germany. An account had to be set up, I needed an Internet and telephone connection, the dogs had to be registered and such mundane questions I could not answer: Where do I toss the empty dog food cans? Where do I get wood, and who will help me stack it in the shed? In the woodpile there was not enough wood to last the winter, and without an internet connection I could not ask Auntie Google where I would find all that was needed.

Luckily the landlady had given me the phone number of her caretaker. She would help me to get everyday things taken care of.

Lisa came to me and we were immediately on good terms. We were about the same age and she had already been warned by my landlady that "a woman from outside" as Germans were called, would rent the whole house alone, which seemed strange here. I was happy that Lisa promised me her help and gladly supported me in finding all the important things. More importantly, she showed me how to start the oven, which was also used to heat the living room. It had a bad draw, so it was difficult to get a steady fire going, an absolute necessity for this house in winter. There was no conventional heating here, to which I was not accustomed, rather there was heating from a stove normally fueled by wood. It would be one of my biggest challenges to keep the house warm, since the stove was never intended to heat the whole house. The hall, the toilet, pantry would always be cold. In the bath there was a radiator, and if it was turned on early enough, it would heat the room reasonably.

My greatest joy was exploring the trails. Here I was able to walk with my dogs as far as our feet would carry us, and choose a new path every day. I postponed completing my to-do list until January, after the holidays, so that I could just enjoy the clear air, the forest trails, the high-altitude paths, and get to know the neighboring villages.

The Flip Side of My Dream

My life in South Tyrol took shape in a tension between the joy of having pursued my dream and the daily challenges that came with living in a wood house at 1,000 meters. I have never frozen so much in my life as I have here. Getting out of the warm bed in the morning required real willpower. Only if the stove was heated and the radiator had heated the bathroom for a while was it bearable and I could prepare myself for the day. And that I could feel lonely, I had not expected. Still, even here, I was tortured by feelings of real loneliness. It was not easy to make friends, as I was used to in Bavaria. The people here were friendly, but it hardly ever came to a more binding exchange. How happy I was that Lisa was an exception: she invited me to dinner at her house, I had her over for coffee, and she suggested we go on a shopping spree sometime. Her husband helped me with the manual work of stacking the wood in the shed after it was delivered, and he was there when something needed to be repaired. This family rescued me several times, for example, when I had lumbago and couldn't move anymore. Without a word, they took care of my pets, brought me food, and drove me to the doctor in Milland. I am eternally thankful to you both!

I enjoyed traveling to Bolzano to experience more Italian flair, to be able to speak Italian, and just to feel like I am living in Italy. Bolzano enchanted me with Italian cafes, the lively Piazza, and the market, where it was nice and Mediterranean: loud, colorful, cheerful. Driving around

Bressanone also excited me. Again and again I thought how privileged I am to live here where other people come for vacation. The Cathedral Square is impressive in its vastness, the mighty Bressanone Cathedral and parish church of St. Michael right next to it. Lining the Piazza are cafes, restaurants, small shops, and of course, "my" real estate office. From here you can reach the absolutely must-see arcades with old, solid buildings, with shops that are adapted to the architecture of the arbors. There are also a few modern shops that do not fit into this venerable ambiance, but now simply belong there.

An Acquisition in Unknown Territory

Although I lived well on my passive income, it was time I thought about how I could open up the country of Italy for myself from here in South Tyrol. My company had opened a location in Italy a few years before, which gave me the opportunity to start my international business here. Yes, I already had some team partners in Austria and even a line in England, but now I had to conquer Italy.

Since I only knew a few people here, it was my first priority to bring myself to life where I could meet people, get to know them, and find those who would like to build an additional income or even gain a foothold in business. So I decided to take part in a dance class, went to a gym, and took interesting courses at the Cusanus Academy.

At the same time I spoke with the family in St. Andrae, who had lovingly received me and treated me like a family member. I learned that in South Tyrol it is customary to have home demonstrations of goods and devices. In Germany home parties were not yet so established and were smiled at as "housewife businesses." So after I showed her my products, I asked Lisa to invite her friends and acquaintances, so I could give a product presentation. To my great joy she agreed and so I was connected to a never ending stream of new contacts. We had a happy evening where again and again I had to vie for the attention of the guests, because the refreshments were Tyrolean bacon, red wine, and a special dry bread, and there was

58

much laughing and storytelling. And in spite of this, or because of it, I made good sales and even received a large order. I was allowed to learn to be relaxed, happy, and less business like. My natural, down to earth nature was very useful to me here. I could just be who I was. Everything artificial and business centered did not function well here. The people saw through it immediately, when you tried to press them to make a decision. But isn't that the case everywhere? Only the South Tyroleans immediately showed their displeasure when they did not like something. An honest man, just expressing his opinion.

New People, New Places

At the dance class I met a nice young woman who also took loving care of me when she recognized me as a "stranger from outside" and offered to show me the sights in the area. Gerti invited me to her home, which I treasured immensely, because I had learned that private invitations of unknown people were not so common in Bressanone. She proudly showed me the Hofburg Brixen, an ornate Renaissance building that until 1972 was the seat of the Bressanone prince-bishops, and that had a very charming inner courtyard. Today, among other things, a crib museum is housed in this sprawling building. Another time we drove to the Trostburg, impressively built on a cliff above Waidbruck, only 20 minutes from Bressanone. Through ongoing renovation this castle is well preserved, and the Trostburg-Tresl leads visitors through the history-laden walls. She is the uncrowned Lady of the Castle, even if she is just a steward. She has spent her whole life at the castle and has many stories about the castle and its counts. A very nice trip, which I enjoyed very much, especially since the road to the castle is of medieval cobblestones and passes through a forest romantically up the mountain. I took several trips with Gerti and we saw each other regularly in the dance class. Unfortunately she did not want to know anything about my products or the business opportunity. It was a pity, but I could see that she was absolutely happy with her life professionally and personally. She just wasn't looking.

And that was the next lesson for me. It was not about finding new business partners, but about being able to offer a chance to people who needed perspective. This does not look so different at first glance, and yet it is a huge difference in attitude and thus also in the result. When I'm looking for new clients and partners to help my business move forward, I use pressure unconsciously and get frustrated about every "no." But if I see myself as a messenger of positive change in one's life, then a rejection is just a no to my offer, not to my self. If a waiter asks me if I'd like more wine and I say No, the waiter doesn't break down in tears!

With this new attitude, I was open to new encounters. When I met people, I listened well to what needs they expressed, to what their wishes were, and simply asked if they were ready for a change. And since I already had some recommendations from my first customers, I was in good spirits and believed in my "Italian success." A very young girl, Angie, was very curious, open minded, and willing to bring something new into her life. She even drove with me to Munich for a three day training, which we both had to explain verbatim to her boyfriend, who didn't want his girl to "travel alone to the big city." But we drove, and also took Lisa along from St. Andrae, as we could stay with her brother-in-law who lives in Munich-Nymphenburg. We were a funny trio, because we each could not be more different. We were united by enthusiasm and we all wanted to do something big. And it really was an exciting experience for my two South Tyroleans, to attend a seminar with over 100 participants, to take part in the exercises, to broaden their horizons and to question established beliefs.

For me it was reviews of the reviews, but still I learned something new, which was because I had grown myself. I had realized my dearest wish to emigrate to Italy. At least I had come as far as South Tyrol and through my frequent trips to Bolzano it felt really Italian for me. These had stretched my mind, opened me up, and made me perceive messages I had not been able to hear before. I had faced my fear and defeated the monster! Yes, that really took me further, in fact, made me bigger and braver. And that's what this seminar was all about: Opening up your own possibilities, which only happens if you think that more is possible, if you tell a new story about yourself. It was not as if I emigrated to the US or to Siberia, but I had broken through my own barriers, and that's what counts. My two companions had also overcome their fear of something new and I was mighty proud of them.

We celebrated this in a big way with a bottle of red South Tyrolean that Lisa had brought, and with her brother-in-law Wolfgang, who clearly felt like a fox in a hen house. We even danced in the large living room of his old, classic apartment. We were crazy funny, happy, and ready to take on the world!

In a café in Milland I met with some interested women whom I had met through my various activities. During sports events, at the dance class, sitting at the café on the splendid Piazza at Bressanone, or simply shopping at the market, I looked everywhere for conversations to get to know people. My target group was women my age, about 50, because I was a familiar contact for talking about particular problems at this time of life. Women over 50

New People, New Places

have the chance to start fresh, to start something new if they put their mind to it. Most of their children are out of the nest, they live on their own terms, and can re-orient their lives. So, it makes sense to take the time to have a review of one's life. What did I achieve? What are my goals? What have I learned? What do I really want to experience? Where does the journey take me next? Unfortunately the view is quite common, that most of your life is over now, that you are no longer needed, and you wrestle with your own self esteem. This is deadly, often in the truest sense of the word, because a person's fear can manifest itself in illnesses, as if it is proof that it will all be over soon.

Regarding this, I remember a funny incident: At a medical massage practice, I lay under an infrared lamp, and followed the conversation in the next room. A woman was lamenting the fate of her friend, whose husband of 40 years had left her. She wouldn't be able to marry again and she would have to carry on all alone. I had just married for the second time at 40 and I burst out laughing. Of course, that was not very sensitive of me, but I couldn't help it.

The first 30 years of life are usually devoted to education and career choice. The next 30 years are for the family, the children, and their education. And now there are 30 very special years: At 60, I have learned a lot, have gained much experience, and now finally know what I want and who I want to be. Thus, the 30 years leading to 90 are particularly exciting and fulfilling, I imagine. In the last 30 years, from 90 to 120, I can enjoy in peace with plenty of time to read, write my memoirs, maybe advise younger people and share experiences from my exciting life, and then go live with my Heavenly Father between 120 and 125. How long I live is out of my hands. But I can be positive. My mantra on this is, "I will be 125 years old, in the best physical, mental, spiritual, and emotional health." This focus may not help me to live that long, but in any case, better, than with a negative attitude, always fearing the worst. I expect the best for myself and my family, and put away unpleasant experiences once and for all, like my second divorce at just under 50. I am grateful for the 10 crazy years with my witty, eloquent husband, and am now ready for new encounters that fit my new life.

A Little Spoiler

As I write I am 64 years old, married for the third time, happy, and excited about my new life. But more on that later.

What Is Your Profession?

I sit in the café and draw circles.

Soon I was known in the café in Milland and received my Latte Macchiato without asking. Here I felt at home, as if in my own living room. Here I listened to the stories of my prospects, offered support where I could, and got to know the life journeys of these women. One of my gifts is that I am immediately at ease with strangers. I just always assume that strangers are people I haven't spoken with yet. As soon as I have a conversation with someone, they are my friend. And in speaking, people feel that goodness, and soon a familiar atmosphere emerges. I truly believe that in the end we are all one. We are all in the same boat, have the same needs, wish for a good life. We all need security, want to be seen and recognized, and don't want to constantly worry about where the money will come from to pay the bills. And when our daily needs are met, we have the wish to leave our footprint, to share our gifts, talents and skills, in order to make a difference. A friend of mine expresses it, "I want to help to make the world a little bit better. It should have been worthwhile for others, that I lived." An idea that pleases and inspires me.

I had started giving seminars at Cusanus Academy in personal development. Mainly for women, I could serve as an example when it came to giving their gifts. I coached women who wanted a career restart because their kids had moved out of the house. They wanted to be more confident.

After years of keeping a household organized, they did not trust themselves to jump headlong back into their one-time professions. It was a great pleasure to work with these women, and to see how they blossomed and ventured back into the professional realm. Some women were also gifted networkers, and collaboration with them began to develop most wonderfully.

The Shock, and Being Done

With my company, I communicated through the Italian Hotline, which was responsible for shipments to Italy as well as events and large presentations there. I befriended Cara, who told me she had settled in well in London and how happy she was to have landed this lucrative job with an international company to support herself and her two children after the unexpected death of her English husband. Though she longed for her Italian homeland, she did not want to make her children leave their home, and above all, she did not want to take them away from their school. She was thrilled about the event in Milan that was scheduled for that summer and we both looked forward to meeting in person to get better acquainted.

Yes, I would be at the event in Milan with my new partners from South Tyrol and they would be able to see the big picture of this global concern, and have the opportunity to get to know the founders of the company. It's always such a great experience to be part of such a company event with your own team members. Nothing is more convincing than seeing with your own eyes and hearing with your own ears what the company is planning, and to experience the new products coming into the market and the vision of the enterprise. Also, such an adventure as this shared trip welds the team together. Shared experiences, new ideas, and newly formed friendships are the motor for greater motivation and the willingness to climb to new heights.

Full of anticipation, we planned the trip, inquired about favorable hotels in Milan, and hatched our own program around the event. Because to be in Milan and not go shopping at the Galleria just wouldn't do. I met with my team regularly to plan new strategies, to find new business partners, and to hold product training. What fun we had! This is work that makes you happy!

But when I wanted to talk to "my" Cara about an order for a new customer, I was told that she no longer worked for the company. I was stunned and sad, because it was clear to me that something unforeseen must have happened. In our last phone conversation we had talked about our meeting in Milan. I did not know at that moment how this "unforeseen" would hit me hard also. As in a trance, I heard that the event in Milan had been cancelled, since the company was no longer serving Italian markets for economic reasons. To my slightly hysterical question as to what that meant, I received the answer, "The Italian market is closed!"

It took me hours to think clearly again. Stunned, I realized the extent of this statement on my life. And the lives of my newly won people! It simply could not be true! That my months-long work was now fruitless, was one realization. But having boarded my people onto a sinking boat, hit me like a bolt from out of the blue. How would I break this to the women who had become my friends? How could I explain that the enterprise in which I had had such trust could make such a consequential decision without any lead-time?

My dream of conquering the Italian market had died. But far worse: my trust in the business had been severely damaged. Yes, actually it had died. For years I had had wonderful experiences with this company. For years, the bonuses arrived punctually in my account. For years, I had celebrated huge successes with my team partners in Germany, Austria, and England. For years, my confidence in this company had grown, I got to know the founders and visited the parent company in California. For years, the successful people in my upline trained me, moved on, and encouraged me to follow them. And now this shock! Yes, maybe the Italian market was not so successful, but could one deny an entire country the chance to become part of the success story? And could they simply pull the rug out from under existing business partners? Thank God I was already successful in other markets, so my bonuses from these markets would continue to flow. But my new partners had invested and now were left standing with products at the close. I would have preferred to secretly disappear out of the dust, but that would not work, and would not be living up to my responsibility to my customers and partners, and it would not be right doing so, because of my high ethic standards. So, I faced the dreadful task and called my team of South Tyrolean and Italian partners to share the terrible news. I was fiercely determined to buy back at least some of the merchandise and to at least offer compensation for the loss of the dream of financial independence. "My people" should not have to suffer a financial loss if they already had to suffer the loss of this precious vision. It was a tearful gathering. Long hugs, uncontrolled sobbing, sharing consolation.

What followed was another nightmare: The uncertainty spread to teams that had nothing to do with the Italian market. I talked to leading people in my upline to get help in this agitated situation. But they also were overwhelmed. Some leaders tried to shrug it off, pointing to success in existing markets, others spoke secretly behind their hands about the demise or survival of the company. It started a real stampede. Some people in my downline blamed me for sinking revenues - they were desperate and didn't know any better. The collapse was huge – in several months sales plummeted and many partners left the sinking ship. To make things worse, the company changed the compensation plan, the sacred cow of network marketing, which was a very bad move for the company. The qualifying sales volume was raised significantly, which meant having to move more goods, in order to keep a qualification that already had been earned. Now the blessing of the auto program became a curse. The company financed a "big car" from a certain level of revenue as a visible sign of success and reward for personal use. And yes, it was a great feeling to speed from Munich to Brixen and back in my Volvo XC 90 and to know that the company would take care of the expensive lease payments. It was the second car I was able to drive at the company's expense. My first car in the program was a Saab convertible, a little dream for me. With my two dogs and my passion for excursions in the mountains, the spacious Volvo 4x4 was more sensible. But as sales dropped drastically, I fell out of the auto program, which meant that I'd have to pay the lease for the remaining three-year period. For a while this was still possible, but the fear was now palpable in my neck, of how long I could still afford all this.

In retrospect I see that I recognized the big crisis of our network company early, because the closing of the Italian market affected me so directly, and it showed me that clearly, something was totally wrong. At the beginning of the collapse, colleagues would scold me as nefarious when I tried to learn more about the background behind this move. To my knowledge, all the executives in my upline left the company. Even the "big ones" who were best able to withstand the financial slump, since the income drop from the six figure range hurt, but stopped falling at a lucrative, bearable level. I would like to report that I dusted myself off and went on to explore new shores. But that was not so – unfortunately! Looking back, I naturally realize that I licked my wounds for too long before I got active again and considered what to do next. I felt dizzy, unable to make a decision, and paralyzed. I never wanted anything to do with network marketing again! Never again did I want to be dependent on company decision on which I had no influence. Never again did I want to look into the questioning eyes of my team members whose questions I couldn't answer. Never again to have anything to do with this crazy world of network marketing.

For months I hid myself at home, went out into nature with my dogs, and prayed that the money would last until I was ready for action again.

What could I possibly do? I had sold my practice, and wondered if I could get the nerve up to build a new practice, considering that I would incur start-up costs, which I definitely did not want. Accept a job? Maybe as a salaried beautician working in a hotel? This would be an unbelievable step backwards, one I would take only as a last resort. I was not afraid of hard work. I had done it all my life. But the freedom I was able to taste in these last years had become so precious to me. To be free to move and be financially free were worth every effort. I would not give up and collect a paycheck working for someone else's dream! I had always been my own boss, except for a brief stint at a freight forwarding company as a young girl. Even then, I resisted unfair treatment, and issued instructions only when I felt they were reasonable. No, this time was not good for me, and not good for my boss! The memory of it not only amuses me today, but also shows me that I really want to live and work independently. I tried out one thing after another, everything possible, and a lot that was "impossible." I was reckless and followed sparkling decoys that promised me the blue from the sky. I was in good company: "Seasoned businessmen" followed the promising idea to build an online publishing house and thus earn the "big money." It was a short dip into the over-the-top lifestyle. Yes, I invested what I had left and was ready to learn and be guided. But soon, the air was let out and the money was gone. Indeed, I was richer for the experience. Crazy as it sounds, I am glad that I tried everything, and that I was prepared to venture into unfamiliar terrain, and to look behind various scenes and realize that even the so-called great ones also cook with water like everyone else.

I always oriented myself too much towards the ostensibly successful entrepreneurial types who dressed well, who could speak well. Anyway, I had grabbed every opportunity to gain experience. It was better than hiding out at home or in the woods. I was alive again, fighting like a lioness, and grasping at all possible straws. In all this chaos, the love of my present husband found me. I had not yet lost my vigor and my positive charisma! He visited me in South Tyrol. We took wonderful mountain tours on the Plose, and exchanged kilometers-long emails during the week. At that time it was still apparent from one's phone bill that one was in love. Germany – Italy phone calls are not cheap! So we decided quickly, very quickly, that we would get together and that I would move back to Bavaria.

Just as I was always willing to take a risk in my professional life, so was I in my private life. I did not regret it. Our first common nest was an uncomfortable, not very charming row house that we left after a year, causing us to move in a short time frame and stirring in me the longing to finally find my home, where I would want to stay put. Back in Germany I made many new contacts, visited network meetings of entrepreneurs, always on the search for new a professional opportunity. Networkers of all stripes wanted to win me over to their companies, but I was not ready to get involved in this industry again. Besides, there was nobody there who was sensitive enough to ask me about my condition. I remember a network colleague who wrote to me via messenger in Facebook, that he had just the right business for me and that I should have a look at the attached presentation. I wrote back to him that I did not want to work with him, even though he had the ideal business for me, because he had not said a word that indicated he was interested in me personally. Just the idea "to get me, the successful networker, into his network" drove him. MLM (Multi-level Marketing) is always a people business. The personal relationship is most important here, the interest in others: First comes the relationship, then the business!

Like before I held seminars at Cusanus Academy in Bressanone, which made me happy, but it was not a lasting solution, as I wanted to live and work in Bavaria. I gave lectures in the Psychological Bookstore in Munich, wrote my first book, "My Rear on the Pack Ice, My Heart in Heaven," the biography of my first 50 crazy years, and was still in the search for my professional El Dorado.

After a lecture an energetic blonde woman came up to me and gave me a big compliment: "You are a very interesting personality – I would like to get to know you better!" That did my unsteady soul some good and I gladly arranged a meeting with her. I did not know that my life would change completely again as a result. The lively blonde visited me at my home in Zorneding and told me about her extraordinary professional career. She was an opera singer but was also looking for a new, lucrative professional challenge and had found it. Now my curiosity was piqued and I wanted to know everything she had to say. Well, I should have known: Again a network marketing business. I expressed my skepticism, told her of my fall from great heights, and my fear of repeated failure, and she listened attentively. She did not push me further, only recommended a product for stress, which I gladly ordered from her. When she was leaving, I asked briefly what I had to do, should I have any interest in joining professionally. Her answer stunned me. "Nothing further. You're already in." Like, "I'm already in it?" After all, I need to sign a contract, read through papers, order a starter package, and know what my initial investment is in order to start my career, right? She said with a wink that I already had the experience in direct sales, but she was working in a pure referral network, and there was nothing I needed to sign, nor any investment to put up. I could contact her again if I wanted to know more. With that she was out the door and I stood, puzzled and speechless, thinking I had misheard her. And I wanted to know more! Of course I did!

For this I arranged an appointment with her in Munich. What I learned from her there once again blew my mind. I allowed myself to lean far outside of my comfort zone and learned that there was a difference between direct selling, something I knew and had worked at, and a pure consumer network.

Multi-level marketing in direct sales

With "my" former company I started with a so-called starter kit, which included the contract to be signed in triplicate, papers regarding the terms and conditions of the business, and catalogs that described the products and their prices. Also included was the license, which you bought from the company. Further, you had to decide on a starter package that included products for your personal use and products for presentations. There were two versions, and of course, the "business version" was recommended. At a cost of 5,000 D-Mark, this is, what I invested in to start my business. From the high investment, I quickly made money, because I duplicated my approach with new prospects, that is, many new partners also got in with the "business version," which in itself immediate bumped up their bonus, interestingly. And this made the approach easier to advertise. At the first level, you got 25%, which meant that selling products was rewarded. Naturally, this investment was not possible for everybody. But since I had no doubt that this investment was worthwhile, I also found suitable prospects who not only wanted to get involved and work together, but who also could afford the business package. What I did not realize at the time was that I always would have to find new partners and rich customers who wanted and could afford these high priced products. It was passive income which was always talked about at business presentations. That would not work for this system, because the bonuses for team building were far lower than those for selling products and for signing up new business package partners. Each time a new product was launched, all the partners were expected to buy the new products, which in turn made the bonus interesting. But a constant effort was required to always find new partners and customers. Team building first brought the great majority of deep partners an interesting monthly bonus check. What was important to understand was that the payout from the deep partners would only be guaranteed with appropriate qualifications, i.e. high personal sales volume and group sales volume (for the first three levels). The size of the team played a secondary roll. Selling was the daily bread! Since these were not consumable products, new customers always had to be found. A sleep system brought in a nice bonus, but lasts 30 years! The filters in water filtration systems had to be replaced every three months, but many customers used the filters longer, or didn't order regularly. Later, our company instituted a monthly subscription system and announced that filters would have to be changed monthly now. That felt weird, even though it was in the company's interest to have a disposable product. These differing statements in product descriptions confused partners as well as customers.

Now I hear from my blonde sponsor that I am "in" with a single order totaling 65 euros, and there is nowhere I need to sign. Also, I did not have to buy any license. And there would be no additional costs at all apart from those of the products I consumed myself. Since I was once used to paying entrance fees to every business meeting, and every training that the company held cost money, sometimes hundreds of euros, I asked in disbelief how this could function.

First, I had to learn the difference between direct sales and referral marketing. Here, in referral marketing, products that are good for you and help you are referred on, and there is a monthly subscription system, since it involves all consumables. Each pack is designed to last a month. There is no distinction between customers and distributors. Anyone who desires a healthy lifestyle will take these vital substances, recommend them to others, and receive a small percentage back as a referral bonus. What I did not understand at first was that at the first level, that is, my partners and customers, there's only a 5% referral bonus. Only if I helped my customers to be successful themselves would I earn more money. So, it was not "to" the people, rather "with" the people. Here team building is clearly rewarded! This is fair! Not selling at any price, but supporting, helping, and promoting your own partners who soon will be using their own products cost-free. What a huge difference! No high monthly costs just to qualify and then having to look for ways to sell all the products. Even today I still own many of the durable products from my first network company, things that were simply too expensive to dispose of. Yes, the products were helpful, but very high priced, and they never were used up. The "new company" even helps new customers quickly refinance their products, with extra bonuses paid to business developers. Starting with just three new customers in the first month, the company offers an additional bonus from an extra pot into which a percentage of the worldwide turnover is fed. Exciting story for me, because I was not used to being supported by the company itself. And further, there is no difference between a customer and a business partner. I can enroll my grandfather and help him grow old well, and he counts on the rewards just as much as the business partner who is interested in building a large team.

Of course, I first had to understand that there is no "get rich quick" scheme being offered here. Because of the low qualification volumes, it takes a while before an interesting monthly bonus check is reached. But exactly that is what gives the assurance that people want to stay in the system, because they have little monthly cost, which they can recoup quickly, and this simply means that people can use their own products for free. And once a team is set up, there is actually something like passive income. Yes, of course I recommend what helps me and does me good and I actively support my team members, helping them to attract and train their new partners. It is a true partnership. The social component is a strong pillar in this business as well as the pillars of health and finance. Where today more and more people are isolating themselves in front of computer screens, and often have so-called friends whom they don't even know personally, the loving, friendly togetherness is an added value that is not to be underestimated.

One study illustrates the importance of social, loving, engaged interaction. Groups of five mice were kept in an ambient environment where they were cared for "normally." So, they received food, water and exercise. In comparison, groups of 25 mice were kept in a so-called "enriched" ambience, meaning that these animals were not only offered food, water, and exercise options, but also toys, hiding places, ways of interacting with other animals, and reward systems.

The mice in the larger social groups, in a stimulating ambience, were many times healthier and longer living than the mice in smaller groups in a normal setting.

We Bavarians have a saying, "Not even in heaven is fun when you're all alone."

In this new referral network, friendships are established easily, as people are not under the enormous stress of reaching their sales numbers. Also, I have never before experienced so many team-wide actions where one supports the other. So, international team building is not only possible, but also highly successful.

What I find even more exciting is that anyone who really wants it, can generate success here. Through the small financial investment, through the simple business model, through the support on the part of the company and that of the upline, it is hard not to become successful unless you just have no incentive to move.

It has been referred to as the "business opportunity for the little guy." And yes, if you compare the different business models with which you can generate an income on your own, referral marketing is by far the easiest system to implement. In a franchise, I have to meet a relatively high investment, and also have to pay monthly fees to the franchisor. In order to open a normal retail store, there are monthly costs for rent and operations, in addition to the initial investment in setting up the site. When I set up my first cosmetic studio as a young woman, I invested little by little a generous amount and could watch monthly as I reined in operating costs. Not to mention the training costs that I invested throughout my career. And now I realize that direct selling – as I said, that was my former company - is not yet the Eldorado of business opportunities, especially when this is more interesting than having to generate high investments and carry ongoing operating costs. Since each consultant buys the products at a discount, then sells them at a premium to end customers, this model skips over the retail business with all its costs like rent, wages and operating costs.

Here – in referral marketing – every person who chooses this healthy lifestyle, buys products at cost, but gets paid a referral bonus for each recommendation. And since the bonus for building teams as well as the success of team partners is many times higher than the sale to end customers, the reward is a real incentive to create a flourishing team. The simplicity of the system promotes duplication, large investments are never required, AND we offer free education and training.

The process is simple and ingenious – I take care of my well-being in that I take sensible, wholesome, vital nutrients. I am then asked what I do to be so fit and healthy and from where I get all my positive charisma. And voila, I have a prospect to whom I can recommend my products. Sometimes I just tell my story when someone asks me what I'm doing for a living. My story is always the same: I have been self-sufficient my whole life and have never thought about my pension. When my 60th birthday approached and I received my pension calculation, I knew that in old age I could not survive on 300 euros. Today I am grateful and glad to have found a system with which I can not only secure a high "pension," and receive unlimited "salary continuation" in case of illness, but rather to be protected by passive income. When I was out for an entire year due to a stroke, I was able to learn how valuable a team in referral marketing really is. I was lovingly supported from all sides, my team rolled up their sleeves and continued to build up the business, supported by my sponsor, who took care of them, fully engaged. I could take the time to get well, learn to speak normally again, and at least not have to worry about financial support. If I think about it, I would not have known where the money would have come from during my sick leave! First I was in the hospital, then for weeks in rehab, and it took a year to practice speaking every day. I went to the speech therapist, the ergonomic therapist, and also had psychotherapy to handle the shock of not being able to speak. Friends of mine said understandably: Laura, and not speaking? That just doesn't fit! The feeling that I was not master of my own body had deeply unsettled me. Today I am restored and can talk again, even if my voice is not as sonorous as before, and I have lost some memories. Sometimes funny situations arise: For 20 years "my girls" and I have been going to the spa in Bad Birnbach and we stay at the Churfuerstenhof. There we enjoy the beautiful hotel-owned spa and sauna, steam room, and special resting space where one can have a light show and a float on a floating couch on which we swing gently back and forth and of course maintain a rain-patter of girl talk. When I was able to travel again a year after my stroke, I discovered a completely new gemstone grotto in the wellness oasis. Excited, I called my girls together and showed them this beautiful new room, which was equipped with a variety of gemstone-studded seat recesses that were wonderfully warmed. The friends looked at each other questioningly and then said very carefully that this room had always existed. I did not believe them. I even went to the reception desk and asked them how long the beautiful gemstone grotto had been there. "About 17 years," was the answer. Names also will escape me, which of course could also have to do with aging. For years I could not say the name of a colleague, someone I especially like. She lovingly started a ritual with me and every time we met, said, "I am Cordula!" But of course these are minimal limitations, and I can live with them. Now I have a good excuse for not being able to calculate well, something I have never been able to do.

I was lucky in misfortune! Not only did I receive the unlimited "continued pay," but after this year my monthly bonus check was 1,000 euros higher than before my illness.

Of course, every partner in the team works for his own benefit, but my friends also knew that they supported me with their own success. Of course I don't wish such an illness on anyone. But in retrospect it was a blessing for me to have decided on this referral marketing model when I did. And since I have a son, it also reassures me that I can bequeath him my business. What good luck!

A Recent Descent Before Victory

I would like to write now, "And my team grew and prospered, the teamwork bore more and more fruit, wonderful friendships were formed, and we all lived happily ever after."

But that's not how it was. Before the success really came (and thank God it was before my stroke) my psyche played crazy again. I feared again that I had ended up in the wrong business, because I was not making money as fast as in my first network, direct sales, where I quickly made good money through the high priced products and my salesmanship. I was distracted by bling-bling offers promising quick money, and tried precious metals sales, which I liked well, because I was dealing in "true value." Looking back, today I do not know what came over me, that I was so unsteady and left my first team partners alone, including my girlfriend from Berlin, who was seriously building a referral business. I was depressive, insecure, volatile, and ran after some idea that promised me the egg-laying, wool-bearing, milk-producing sow. it does me no honor to admit that, but I hope it will serve you when you read it.

I disappointed the first leadership of the company, who invited me to Mallorca for a whole week to introduce me to the referral model, and to support me, to process my bad experience, and to instill hope in me that I would become a good team partner. Everything was "too good to be true" for me, as I had never experienced such caring for the last ten years, not even from my former upline. My cosmetics client, who became my sponsor, never worked the business self-sufficiently. She benefitted from my success, which I begrudged her, because I was so happy that she had brought me into this exciting networker life. She could even afford a condominium in Munich, which I thought was great, but could not ever support my business. The other upline was located in the north of Germany, so we had not only spatial distance. So, I was used to hammering on, learning from books, listening to a lot of CDs on the subject, and just putting all my courage together and just doing it. I had the definite will to succeed and that's why it worked. I had to lick my wounds a little longer, "nurture" my sacrificial existence, and sink so low that I accepted an invitation to "the week of faith" from Karl Pilsl in Austria's Mill Quarter. I had no idea what to expect there. I followed my intuition and asked my husband to go there with me, because health-wise, it was not a good idea for me to make this long trip alone.

What I experienced there was quite unexpected. I knew Karl Pilsl for ten years, recognized him as a keynote speaker at several events where he talked about economics, nature-compliant strategies, and political issues as well as his experience in America and Europe, the two worlds where he lived.

Now he talked about faith, quoted the bible, and for the first time I heard that Jesus did not come to found a religion, but to have a relationship with his people. And that it's not about what **I** accomplish, but what Jesus did for me and whether I am willing to accept it. This exploded my understanding of everything I had read and heard about the church and faith. I had left the church, because I could not find a spiritual home in the Catholic nor the Evangelical church. I sought my fortune in esotericism like so many people do today, ordered the universe, had my tarot cards read, adjusted to the cycles of the moon and read my horoscope, leaving no stone unturned to find my happiness and to master my fate. Now I learned from Karl Pilsl that Jesus brought freedom! Freedom from any yoke, and that his call in the bible appears in Galatians 5:1 – Christ has released us to freedom. Stand firm therefore, and *do not let yourself again put on a yoke of bondage.* And what a yoke was laid before me in the name of God: You must do this, you must not do that, and if.... then! Everything threatening and not suitable for finding your own happiness. I also understood that I order all things according to the creator, rather than the universe, which is also His creation. Everything was very surprising for me. What was even more surprising was that when I was crying out to Karl how insecure I was and did not know what I should do professionally, he answered me: "How dumb can you be to take the products of this wonderful company in referral marketing for so long and to not work the related business." When I asked him if he would advise me to get involved in this business after all I had experienced, a clear message came, "Yes!" I was not healthy, everything was too much for me, and I went to bed in my hotel room. Here I prayed with supplication and crying: God, if you really exist, and love me as Karl said, then please, please give me a sign as to what I should do." That night I had a fever, tossed back and forth in bed and had confused dreams. In the morning I had my requested sign: I was very healthy, fit, felt terrific and full of energy. All the tribulation was blown away, all my depressed feelings disappeared, and I was filled with a clarity that had not been seen for a long time. My husband, who had to experience my mood swings for a long time, was more than amazed to see me so happy and solid after this troubled night. This was clearly a miracle! I ran to Karl to tell him how much my point of view had changed overnight. Not deeply impressed, he said only, "God can supernaturally affect everything." The work had only just begun, but now I was strengthened, had seen light at the end of the tunnel, so a real perspective! I realized, "When perspective wakes, despair goes to sleep." First and foremost I was able to apologize to my team partners, especially my girlfriend from Berlin, as well as my sponsor, who lovingly and committedly cared for my people at this time when I was absent.

And Once Again, My New Life

I was allowed to recognize: "God helps always, and at the latest, right on time" if I turn to HIM, believe HIM. As long as I trust in "things" and man-made ideologies, HE, a complete gentleman, leaves me alone. That is the story of free will. I have told where my thick head led me, and it was not always easy for me and others to bear the consequences.

I am very grateful that a highly esteemed fellow couple (when I was not yet a "real" colleague) took me to Houston Texas, to Lakewood Church, a former 12,000 seat sport stadium with an estimated 15,000 visitors. Here I was allowed to hear such encouraging words that showed me that God is so different from what they tried to tell me in my childhood. God loves his people. He is a generous, benevolent father. We can come to Him for everything and He always helps us with everything. Often not as we imagine, but always in the perfect way. When Joel Osteen, pastor of Lakewood Church, was accused of preaching a prosperity gospel, he asked what else he should preach. And yes, I was allowed to experience God as wonderfully generous. He is happy to fulfill the wishes of his children, who entrust themselves to Him. I often hear Joel Osteen's encouraging lessons via YouTube, and can only tell you how they inspire me.

Meanwhile, I do what God doesn't do and God does what I can't do.

So I have become completely healthy: with trust in God, discipline and vital substances such as special micronutrients for the brain.

For me it is a miracle that the fear has disappeared, the depression belongs to the past, and today I have the certainty that I have landed in the right company and have found my professional home. In addition I have found the right nutrition with which I can feast while remaining slim, fit, and healthy. My company offers high quality and specially formulated micronutrients and superfoods geared toward disease prevention, enabling people to live long and healthy lives. As the so-called geriatric diseases such as dementia and Alzheimer's disease increase at a frightening pace, I am happy that I can provide a degree of prevention with the appropriate "brain food."

In the past I did not know what improvements could be made in this area.

Another issue is maintaining the ability of cells to duplicate in a healthy manner. For scientists, a wide ranging field of research. For me, simply the possibility to do everything in order to grow old healthy.

I have to laugh at the saying, "Nobody wants to grow old, but nobody wants to die young." No, not me either. I'd rather keep an image of myself as a wise, witty old woman. And until then I believe God has some plans for me.

I earn enough money to book seminars all over the world, like in 2018, at the 4-day High Performance Seminar by Brendan Burchard in Phoenix, Arizona.

And probably the best profit is that I have enough time for me. I always love being able to go out in nature every day, to be able to dedicate myself to my hobbies, writing books, playing the piano, and mountaineering, as well as attending trainings, which is simply my great passion. For example I graduated 2017-2018 with Veit Lindau as a certified Integral Life Coach and Human Teacher, which is inspiring, because I can always help people avoid some of the detours that have cost me a lot of strength, time, and money. Additionally, I am taking a 1000-day challenge with Brian Johnson, from 4/6/2017 to 1/1/2020, during which I train with beneficial thoughts daily. Today I am at Impulse No. 770 and I can say that my life has changed positively. It is mainly about making your own daily routine consciously health-promoting, and aligning your own mindset positively. And I do this in small steps, as described in the book by Jeff Olson, "Slight Edge: The Small Lead," which I read enthusiastically. That's how I took my small steps fitness program, by completing a 15 minute workout daily, Monday through Friday. This is a manageable amount of time that I can take daily. And yet 56 hours come out over the weeks and months at the end of the year, although I have already deducted vacation time. This is how every great endeavor works. My Jakobsweg of 1,000 kilometers through Spain started with the first step. My team started with the first phone call and continuing conversations. Following the motto, "Daily two, I'm in!" This way, every goal is attainable. Small steps, continually taken. This continuity is what leads to success. Stay tuned! The slowest, who keeps on going, is faster than the sprinter who gives up on the track.

My greatest happiness is that today, after 30 moves, I finally found my home. I live in Hammer, in beautiful Chiemgau. Every day I thank God for this beautiful place where I have a real sense of home and was able to meet very lovely, open people who accept me as I am. "I am Laura – and here I belong!" It would fill a separate book to describe the path I took until I landed here. In any case I was protected and guided and am able to enjoy this daily, my very personal miracle. Here I offer not only individual coaching, which of course is also possible on the phone, where each conversation is available in recorded form, but also mastermind groups for people who want to live their genius, and talk circles on topics on God and the world.

Within the Academy of Fortune Research, of which I am president, I show ways to achieve happiness.

My wonderful referral marketing company takes very good care of all partners who are serious about team building.

This is how I have been able to enjoy many trips and get to know my company up close, be it in England, where the European headquarters are, or in the USA at the parent company.

Every year senior executives get together with the company's founders and take a cruise, which I have been able to experience for the fifth time this year. It is a wonderful journey where I am able to gather new impressions, make new friends and broaden my horizons, experience new things, and learn how to support people to reach their goals.

The swarm intelligence of a large network is an added asset, and there is virtually nothing that cannot be helped by someone in the group.

I could recognize that the feeling of deep fulfillment in life is not from bling-bling, but from the giving of one's gifts, talents and abilities for the benefit of all.

I am now 64 years old and I am looking forward to the next 60 years, which I can live with the feeling of Having Arrived, God willing. I have acquired a lot of experiences that can help people, and so today I am experiencing happiness for being there for people who want to make more of their lives, venturing out of the normal life of limitation and scarcity, and longing for a fulfilled life with abundance, joy, freedom and peace with good friends who selflessly and lovingly ask that anyone who wants it can find his ingenuity.

My affirmation: "I will be 125 years old, in the best mental, physical, spiritual, and emotional health, God willing." And if I have only one more year to live, I would want to live it the way I do now: Fulfilled, grateful, and dedicated to the wellbeing of "my people."

Thank You

Thank you for having followed me to this point. I wish with all my heart that you dare to live your greatness, and that you dare to try out new things. We are all in one boat, inhabiting this single beautiful earth, which we should take good care of. Let's change the world together, starting with ourselves.

I like the thought: "God's love is expressed through the gifts and talents He gave us." Our thank you to Him is that we live our talents and gifts and share these with others.

In deep unity,

Yours, Laura

PS: My new book named,

"Your Radiant, New I."
Seven proven steps into a joyful, self-determined life

will be helpful for you!

Extract of "Your Radiant, New I"

Description of the Book

Personality development through methods that are implemented in small steps, and that bring a light into your life. You will have more energy, more joy, and so more charisma. It will draw in success to all areas of your life. You will achieve more, and simply be happier. As soon as you have thrown out the procrastination and "postpone-mentitis" from your life, you will say with an erect posture and sparkling victory in your face to your life's demands: Bring them on! This is my experience from implementing these steps.

By Laura Milde

Clarity about what you want

The reason we do not attain clarity about what we truly want deep in our hearts is based on many different fears.

Of these, the primary fear is of failure. If I am nobody special, then nothing can go wrong. This is true, but it is an insufficient defense. I always live below my possibilities, and the worst part of this is that I know it, and knowing it makes me feel bad about it.

Are you familiar with the fear of being successful? It sounds really weird, doesn't it?! And yet this fear is another drag on our path to our inner genius. If we imagine ourselves succeeding beyond measure, the way we have long dreamt it in bold daydreams, the judicial authority in our minds steps in and asks if we have gone completely out of our minds. Because great success is always for others, for those who have earned it, but not for me! And besides, I can't exalt myself over my friends or wherever possible over my own family, right? That would be very wicked, says your inner judge. Or are you not familiar with that? Lucky you!

Well maybe you are familiar with this:

The fear of showing yourself

It is the simple distinction between who you are and who you are not. Between all you know and all you have no idea about. This is especially intimidating, and therefore a popular escape is just not to show yourself. And so all your special gifts and talents and capabilities remain in the drawer where they help no one, neither you nor anyone else.

PPS: Please address your questions truthfully, who recommended you the book - he certainly hopes that this information is valuable to you!

PPS: If you want to know more about my adventures: "The Bottom on the Pack Ice, the Heart in the Sky," a biography that encourages (available in German only at the moment).

Here I have openly and completely told of my crazy, sometimes "crime-related" first 50 years of my life.

Liability Exclusion

The author reserves the right not to be responsible for the topicality, correctness and completeness of the information provided in this work. Liability claims against the author, which refer to material or immaterial nature, which were caused by the use or disuse of the information provided or by the use of incorrect and incomplete information, are excluded, unless the author proves intentional or grossly negligent Fault is present.

All offers are non-binding. The author expressly reserves the right to change, supplement or delete parts of the pages or the entire offer without prior notice or to stop the publication temporarily or permanently.

www.ingramcontent.com/pod-product-compliance
Lightning Source LLC
Chambersburg PA
CBHW072227170526
45158CB00002BA/784